CASHOLOGY ACADEMY WEALTH WORKBOOK

Develop The Proper Money Habits That Lead To Financial Success

Hasheem Francis & Deborah Francis

CASHOLOGY ACADEMY's Mission is: *To Change The Money Chaser To A Money Master Through Wealth Building And Economic Wellness.*

Copyright © 2012 by **CASHOLOGY ACADEMY.** All rights reserved. Distribution and reproduction are strictly prohibited by law. All Scriptures are from the King James Version, unless otherwise noted.

No part of this publication may be reproduced, stored in a retrieval system, or transmitted in any form, or by any means, electronic, mechanical, photocopying, recorded, scanning, or otherwise, except as permitted under Section 107 or 108 of the 1976 United States Copyright Act, without the prior written permission of the publisher or author. Requests to the authors should be addressed to **CASHOLOGY Company:**

info@BTPCompanies.com

For information about reprints rights, translation, or bulk purchases, please contact info@BTPCompanies.com or you can write to CASHOLOGY COMPANY, LLC, and P.O Box 552, Plymouth, FL 32768

Develop The Proper Money Habits That Lead To Financial Success

Produced by: CASHOLOGY ACADEMY
Written by: Hasheem Francis & Deborah Francis
Cover design by: BTP Marketing Group
ISBN: 0615647464
Published by: BTP Publishing, LLC, Plymouth, FL

Disclaimer

The information contained in this material is for information purposes only.

Built To Prosper Companies or CASHOLOGY ACADEMY does not hold itself out as providing any legal, financial or other advice. Built To Prosper Companies or CASHOLOGY ACADEMY also does not make any recommendation or endorsement as to any investment, advisor or other service or product or to any material submitted by third parties or linked to this material. In addition, Built To Prosper Companies or CASHOLOGY ACADEMY does not offer any advice regarding the nature, potential value or suitability of any particular investment, security or investment strategy.

The product and services mentioned in this book may not be suitable for you. If you have any doubts you should contact an independent financial advisor. In particular some of the investments mentioned may not be regulated under the Financial Services Act 1986 or at all and the protection provided to you under this Act will not apply.

We make financial suggestions and it is up to you to make your own decisions, or to consult with a registered investment advisor when evaluating the information of Built To Prosper Companies or CASHOLOGY ACADEMY.

CONTENTS

Take Responsibility For Your Financial Future 11

Finding Your Financial Self.. 13

7 Steps To Financial Freedom.. 19

Your Money Habits.. 23

Your Financial Success Is In Your Hand.. 24

The 10 Cash Only Commandments Of Money.. 27

Know Thy Cash flow... 31

Know Thy Assets And Liabilities... 33

Tracking Your Use Of Money... 35

Saving Accounts... 42

Applying The Wealth Principles Of The Money Masters.............................. 55

50 Ways You Can Earn Additional Income.. 57

Your Money Experience... 61

Building Your Credit History... 69

Using Credit: Other People's Money... 71

Home Ownership... 73

Buying A Car... 77

Financial Terms.. 79

Authors.. 93

Resources.. 95

TAKE RESPONSIBILTY FOR YOUR FINANCIAL FUTURE

You need to start thinking about living financially-smart. If you rely too much on credit for support, you have to draw a line, one that you will not be tempted to cross easily. You have to put an end to your dependence on credit cards, because in the long run, you will find yourself with insurmountable debt.

Be wise. Money must be managed well. Sure, the credit companies will not go away. Years from now, they will still be around, willing to give you credit. They are always there but take the initiative to not associate your issues with them. You do not need to waste a cent to cover unnecessary services or fees.

It is all about strategically using your wealth. Management is the key. You have to think about your future. Not using a credit card has its perks in more ways than one. You learn how to keep yourself grounded by having limitations on what you buy. By not using a credit card means you use cash for your purchases. You can only purchase the items that you have the cash for at that time and nothing more.

Many argue that since they work hard, they deserve to get whatever they want. But if you have to use credit cards for those desires, then you are living outside of your means and you are purchasing those desires on credit. Finance companies and banks will offer you money but eventually you will have to pay for what has been borrowed. You will not be aware of it but the charges and fees will be taking more money out of your pocket.

At first, you may find it quite painful to not be free to buy whatever you want. Overtime, if you are smart with your money through saving and investing then eventually you will be able to pay for what you want with cash. Be patient because in the long run, you will be proud of yourself for having control over what you can do with your money.

Do not be harsh on yourself. If you want something, reward yourself. Just be sure you have the cash with you to pay for what you buy. The key is to create a cash only lifestyle.

The goal is to achieve financial freedom, free from debt and overcoming the fear of paying your bills. It is not suggested that instead of owning credit cards, you load up your wallet with a bundle of cash. Of course, you can use checks and debit cards if there is a certainty that you have the funds to cover the transactions. There is no better time to start having the best interest of your future in mind than now.

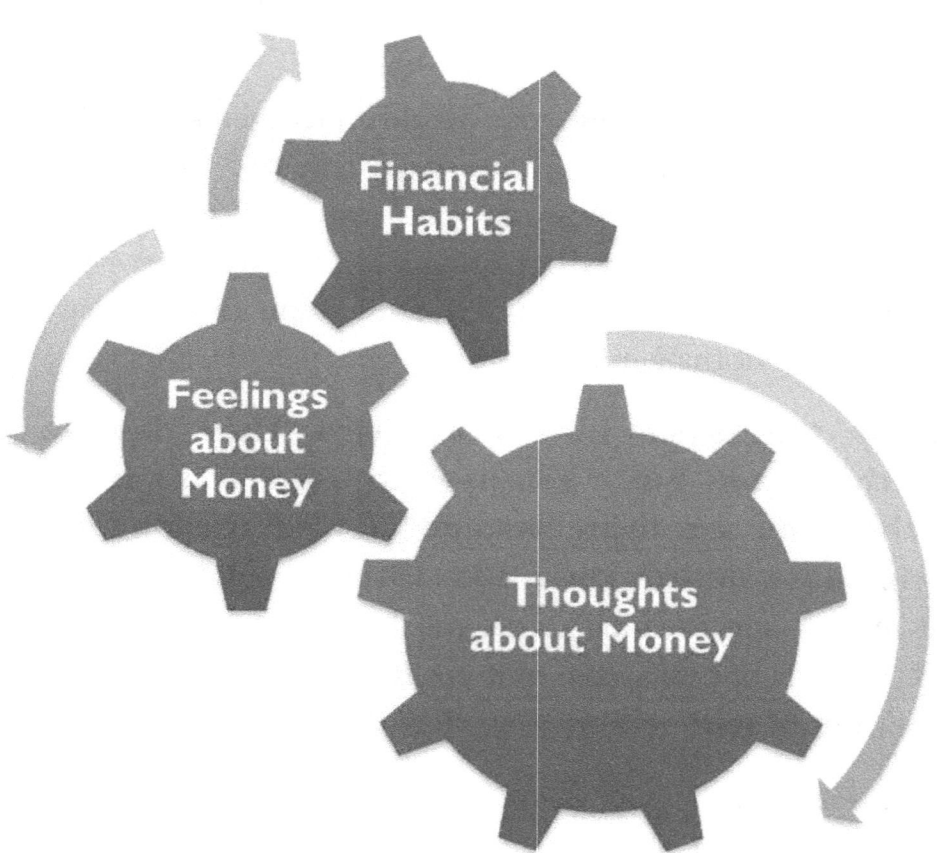

FINDING YOUR FINANCIAL SELF

To help you identify your beliefs about money, take a few moments to complete the following sentences:

My parents beliefs about money are: _____
_____
_____
_____
_____
_____

The things I have learned about money from my parents are: _____
_____
_____
_____
_____
_____

The phrase I heard most often growing up about money is: _____
_____
_____
_____
_____
_____

When discussions about money come up at home, I feel: _____
_____
_____
_____
_____
_____

I often get overwhelmed about money when: _____
_____
_____
_____
_____
_____

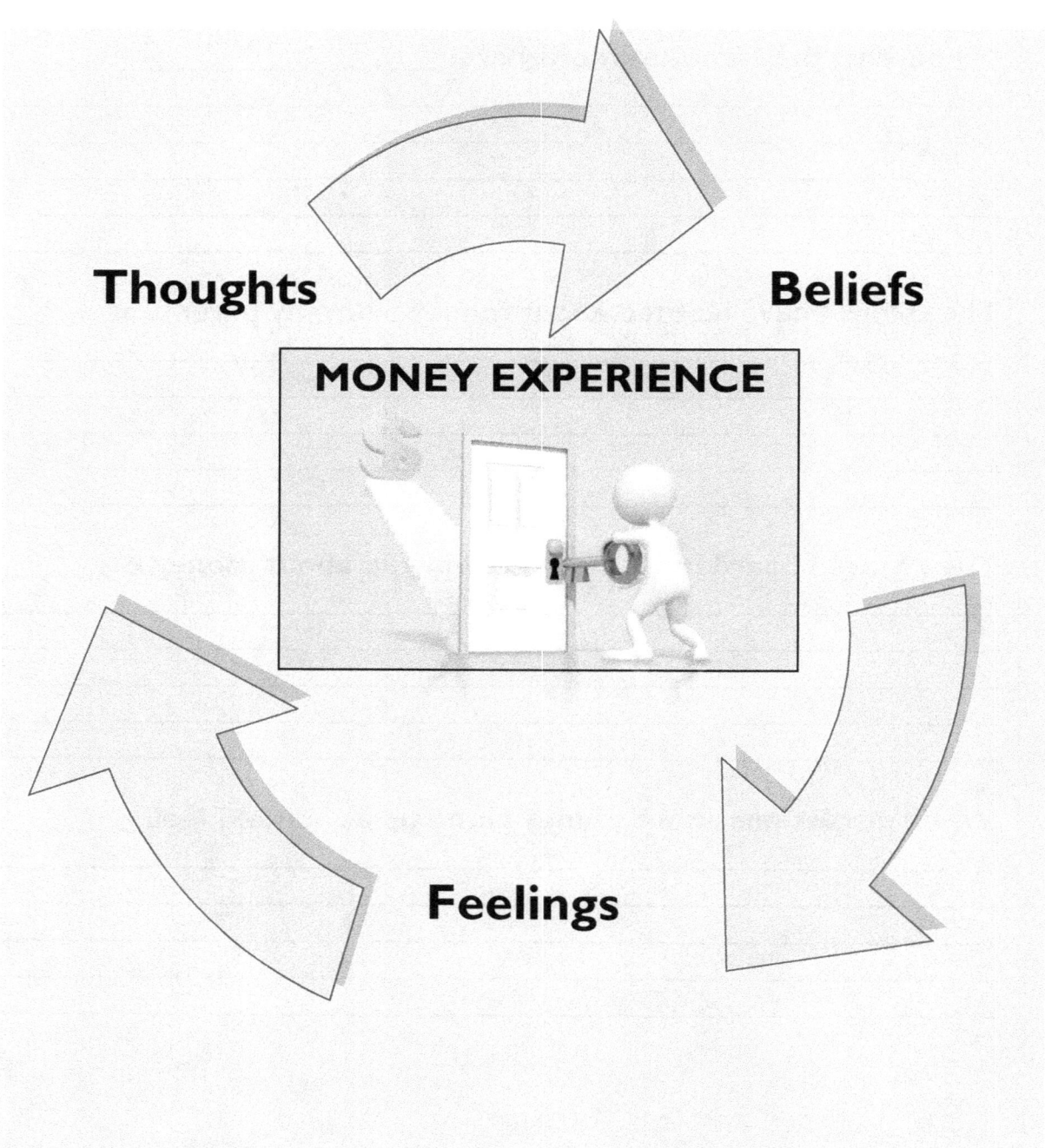

How would you describe your current belief toward money?

Do you feel you deserve to be wealthy and provided for? Or are you afraid of wealth?

What specific financial goals have you established for your life? Do you know your financial freedom number?

7 STEPS TO FINANCIAL FREEDOM

7 Steps to Financial Freedom

Here is a seven-step goal-setting exercise that you can use to set and achieve your financial goals. These action steps summarize the best techniques for setting goals, streamlining your activities, and enabling you to accomplish vastly more than the average person.

Step 1: Know Your Financial Freedom Number.

You need to know exactly what amount you need coming in on a monthly basis passively that would give you financial freedom. Write down a specific dollar amount that you feel you will need to live a comfortable life. For example, if it is $250,000 per year you need then set it and do not deviate from it. Sit down and create a list of your expenses, so you can have a clear picture of where most of your income is going. The goal is to increase not decrease your income.

Step 2: Have A Reason "Why" And Know How It Would Make You Feel To Achieve Your Financial Goal.

Your reason "Why" must be much bigger than just paying your bills. Your why must motivate you, because you must become more to earn more. It will be a process you must go through before you achieve your goal. If you have the expectation to be a millionaire, know that it is going to take some time especially if you have never earned more than $100,000 dollars in a given month or year.

Step 3: Evaluate The Obstacles That You Will Have To Overcome To Achieve Your Financial Goal.

Once you decide to be free and take consistent and persistent action, there will be obstacles you will need to overcome. For example, if you are a compulsive spender, stay away from the local shopping malls until you overcome your spending habits. Eliminate any self-defeating obstacles that will hinder you from achieving your goal. Stick to your commitment.

Step 4: You Will Need The Proper Tools That Will Empower You To Have The Skills And Abilities To Reach Your Financial Goal.

In order to achieve a financial goal you have never reached before, you must become someone you have never been before. You must develop knowledge and skills that you need to become a money master. Jim Rohn, America's foremost business philosopher said, *"After you become a millionaire, you can give all of your money away because what's important is not the million dollars; what's important is the person you have become in the process of becoming a millionaire."* Every new goal requires that you become a new person, in some way, by developing additional knowledge and skills in order to achieve the level of success that you desire.

Step 5: Evaluate Your Associations. The People You Surround Yourself With Will Determine If You Achieve Your Financial Goal.

To achieve financial freedom requires the active cooperation of many people. Remember, it is all about relationships. Seek out those who have already achieved financial freedom. Do not be afraid to ask for help, even if it is in the form of advice and introductions from the people you know. One person, one contact, can make all the difference between success and failure.

Step 6: Create A Plan To Achieve Your Financial Goal.

Put your plans in writing and review it daily. Your plan becomes your compass to keep you on track. Create a list of your financial obligations. Organize the list into a plan based on priority and sequence. Everyone's financial freedom goal might be slightly different. Some might be content with their finances but are failing to plan for their children's college education, or put aside money for their 401k or retirement. Whatever your inner voice is telling you to improve on is what needs to drive your passion.

Step 7: Take Action!

Once you begin, never stop. Do something every day that moves you toward the achievement of your financial goal. Develop a bias for action and a sense of urgency, consistently moving towards your goal. Do whatever is necessary, once you begin working on your goal; never stop until you achieve it. Get the results you desire.

To accelerate the process of achieving your financial goal, create a clear mental picture of what your goal would look like as if you had already achieved it. Begin with the end in mind.

Visualize and imagine your goal as a reality. Imagine the feeling of pride and satisfaction you would enjoy if the goal were already accomplished. Most importantly journal your experience on the road to achieving your financial goals. Then you will have a blueprint for others to follow. This will change your family's legacy.

In setting financial goals, your main job is to be absolutely clear about what it is you want. Develop a plan to achieve that goal, and work on it every single day. Remember, there are no limits except the limits you place on your own imagination.

YOUR MONEY HABITS

Take the money mastery self-evaluation and answer honestly.

True False   I deserve to be wealthy.

True False   I am a great money manager.

True False   I know the difference between an asset and a liability.

True False   I track my monthly cash flow and expenses.

True False   My financial future is secure.

True False   I manage debt well.

True False   I have a plan to pay off all of my debt.

True False   I have a savings, investing and a vacation account.

True False   I invest in my financial education monthly.

True False   I give 10% of my income to a charity of my choice.

True False   I save at least 20% of my income.

True False   I am not a compulsive spender.

True False   I know my financial freedom number.

If you answered **True** to most of the questions, you are controlling your money well. If you answered **False** to three or more questions, you may want to make some changes.

○ INVESTING

○ SAVING

○ LEARNING

YOUR FINANCIAL SUCCESS IS IN YOUR HAND

We get in life whatever we concentrate upon. Our financial success or financial failure is in our own hands. Many who are complaining that the door to financial success is locked by some mysterious rich person, or they have no one to help them to get the position they desire, are not succeeding financially because they are not willing to make the necessary effort to succeed. They are not willing to do the work required; they want someone else to do the work for them to make things happen. Through my experiences in life I have seen people who dreamed big but failed to live out those dreams due to their halfhearted commitment to the process of developing themselves. Equally as important is the people that you surround yourself with. My mentor said; *"He could see my financial future just by looking at the five people with whom I spend the most time with."*

To create wealth you have to learn how to have self-control and live within your financial means and invest wisely. If you study the money habits of those  who are wealthy, you will see a pattern. They only "use" other people's money to acquire assets such as real estate, or businesses. This asset will pay back the money which was used initially and they will continue to earn income from that investment. In Robert Kiyosaki's bestselling book; **Rich Dad Poor Dad** he stated; "concentrate your efforts on only buying income-generating assets." **Key principle: Whatever you do with borrowed money, should make YOU more in income and interest than what you have to pay to the lender.**

When you shift your mindset from a consumer to a wealth builder you change the money game to a new set of rules. When the rules of the game about money changes, your whole world starts changing. When you transform your thinking, you transform your world. **There are no limits to you attaining your most desired financial goals as long as you can**

define what it is you want to achieve. A great deal of what you have perceived as limits in your financial life are actually limits you have placed upon yourself. The good news is you have already begun to eliminate these limits. You began the moment you picked up this book. This book will help you address your money habits directly.

Challenge and change your mental programming. The secret to success is the mind can accomplish whatever it believes. To be a smart Money Master, you must think like one. Do not follow the path of those who blame everyone else for their financial woes and make excuses rather than take personal responsibility for their finances. Excuse makers who choose not to face their problems and their view about finances create a distorted view of life which causes them grief.

There are people who live according to the wealth building principles, but there are an increasing number of people who lack the basic financial life skills and it is ruining their lives. Financial wisdom and the proper use of money is the key to creating a prosperous lifestyle.

Wealth begins not in a bank but in your mind. It begins with your thoughts. Throughout this book we are going to be working on your thinking. No one can think for you, all we can do is provide the necessary tools and it is our responsibility to take the steps to utilize them. To be successful at anything in life you must develop the right attitude. You may face some obstacles or setbacks but it is through your persistence and faith that you will achieve your financial goals. **CASH ONLY is not only a mindset, it is a lifestyle.** You can quote affirmations all day, but it will not work without taking action. In James 2:17 of the Bible it states, "Faith without works is dead." It requires work to succeed.

THE 10 CASH ONLY COMMANDMENTS OF MONEY

Commandment I
Know Thy Source. "Remember the LORD your God, for it is he who gives you the ability to produce wealth." When you are elevated financially, remember where your blessings come from. Avoid arrogance and be humble and grateful. Do not put your trust in money, but in the Living God.

Commandment II
Master Thy Servant (Money). Never allow money to decide what you can and cannot do. The first place to master money is in your mind. Wealth is created mentally; it is thought out before it becomes a reality. Have a positive attitude toward money, never allow money to 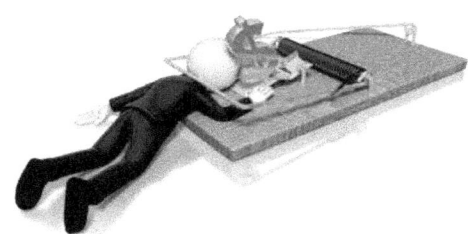 determine what you can and cannot do. If you think too much about the lack of money, or too much about your debt, your thoughts will tend to bring to you the very thing you are trying to get away from. You can attract what you desire as easily as you can attract what you hate. You can only rise and conquer your finances by lifting up your thoughts.

Commandment III
Have A Storehouse To Manage Your Money. In order to manage your money, you need a storehouse. Carefully selecting a financial institution is probably the most important part of the process. Selecting a bank that is  a bad fit for your financial growth could mean you have to start your search all over again in a few months. The search should start with looking at what your priorities are for a checking account. Bank with an institution that values you as a client.

Commandment IV

Know Thy Assets and Liabilities. Assets increase in value, liabilities decreases in value. An asset puts money into your pocket, an asset should generate income on a regular basis. Liabilities are the opposite of assets. Liabilities take money out of your pocket. Work to increase your assets and decrease your liabilities. Know the difference between good and bad debt. What is good debt? *When you use OPM (other people's money) to invest in an asset that provides a cash flow to pay back the debt, put money in your pocket and increase in value.* These forms of debt "usually" have low interest rates and therefore can be maintained for long periods of time as you build up your assets. Bad debt includes debt you have taken on for things you do not need or cannot afford and decrease in value. The worst form of bad debt is consumer credit cards since they usually carry the highest interest rates. Interest rates for credit cards can far exceed even the best investments which would negatively impact your overall cash-flow and net worth.

Commandment V

Know Where Thy CASH Flows. Measure your cash flow by tracking your weekly and monthly expenses vs. your weekly and monthly income. Review your monthly bank statements, know where thy cash is coming from and going. Take advantage of a number of services offered by your bank, including direct deposit and automatic bill pay. Make the most of on-line banking. To make tracking your expenses easy and accurate, pay for everything with cash, check, or debit card. Grow your income more quickly than your expenses, so that each year you can devote more resources toward your long-term goals.

Commandment VI
Learn From Thy Fellow Money Masters. Seek out a mentor, someone who has already Mastered Money.

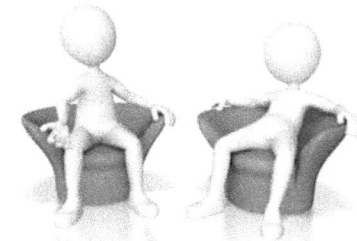

Having mentors who have achieved success in their life is important to your success. Many have already traveled the road you may be on. I remember the advice from my mentor "Always learn from other people's mistakes and their successes. It will save you time and money." Learn from those who have what you want. Be a student of the financial game. Consider joining with other Money Masters either in an internet community (CASH ONLY Community) or in a physical community. Others with a similar mindset as your own can go a long way when it comes to helping you learn new financial skills, build your strength, and identify and remove your weaknesses. Read investing books, read the annual reports of the companies in your portfolio, and pay some attention to news in the world of finance.

Commandment VII
Know Thy Friends. Do not waste your time discussing finances with

anyone who is not supportive of your financial education. You must stand on guard at the door of your thoughts; keep out all the enemies of your happiness and achievement. "The less you associate with some people, the more your life will improve. Any time you tolerate mediocrity in others, it increases your mediocrity." Colin Powell

Commandment VIII
Multiply Thy Streams of Income. Do not rely on one stream of income. If that one stream dries up it can put you in a financial bind. Creating multiple streams of income ensures you will always be earning income. Creating multiple streams of income requires time, education, work, and commitment. If you want to earn more, work less, and have financial freedom, you are going to have to start creating income streams that do not require your direct involvement. You want financial freedom as well as time freedom.

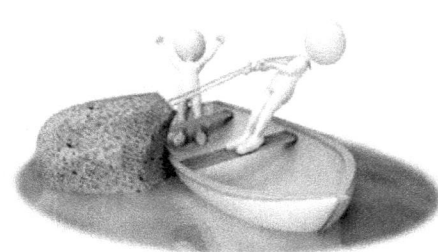

Commandment IX
Owe No Man. The rich rule over the poor, and the borrower is servant to the lender. When you develop the habit of always borrowing money, you come into a position where you are known as a leech.

Commandment X
Spread the Wealth. Anything you hoard and keep that should be shared becomes your god. Be generous! Wealth should be shared on a consistent basis to help out with a worthy cause. When we are wealthy, our blessing is to be a blessing to others. You can never consider yourself wealthy if you do not have the heart to be generous with your money. "As you give, so shall you receive." If you do not sow, you cannot reap. In all of life, receiving depends upon giving.

KNOW THY CASHFLOW

Budgeting is the most important thing you can do to help you achieve your financial goals. There are people who earn plenty of money but are broke, because they do not manage their money well. The key is to be disciplined in your money habits. You must create a plan and stick to it.

My Income	My Expense
Earned Income $	Rent/Mortgage $
Business Income $	Property taxes/Insurance $
Interest $	Internet $
Dividends $	Cable $
Residual Income $	Car Payments $
Bonus $	Car Insurance $
Commissions $	Other loan payments $
Real Estate Rentals $	Health insurance $
IRA $	Day care/Elder care $
Life Insurance $	Gas/Oil $
Other $	Water $
	Telephone/Cell phone $
	Grocery $
	Transportation/Gas $
	Car maintenance $
	Education $
	Personal expenses $
	Other $
Total Income $	**Total Expenses $**

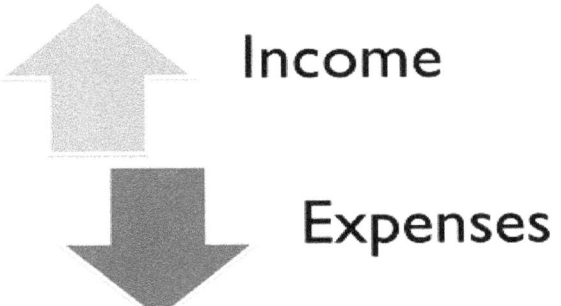

Income

Expenses

DEVELOP THESE MONEY HABITS

- Get in the habit of paying yourself first.
- Keep a log of your daily expenditures.
- File your receipts on a monthly basis.
- Learn to balance your checkbook.
- Begin paying for things with cash.
- Save to buy big ticket items.
- Evaluate your financial statement.
- Pay off any credit used on a monthly basis.
- Put yourself in a position to have interest work in your favor and not against you.
- Have your money working for you, bringing in more money.

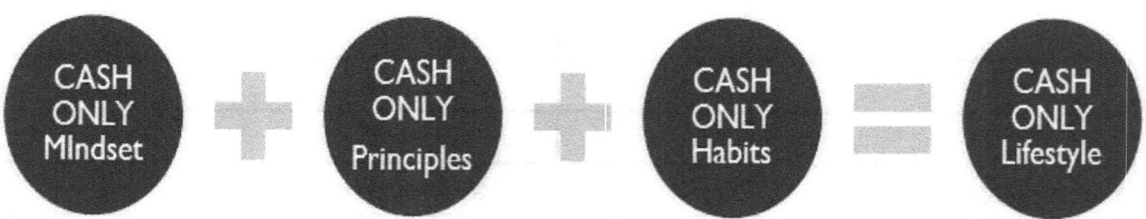

KNOW THY ASSETS & LIABILITIES

Your first step to financial freedom is to find out where you are. Write down all your assets, list everything you own. To begin any worthwhile journey you must know where you are departing from.

Assets − Liabilities = Networth

Assets

Liquid Cash	$
Checking	$
Savings	$
CD's	$
Money Market	$
Treasury Bills	$
US Savings Bonds	$
Cash Flow Real Estate	$
Gold	$
Gold Coins	$
Silver	$
Platinum	$
Retirement	$
TOTAL ASSETS	$

LIABILITIES

List all of your liabilities. Put down everything you owe. Once you have your assets and liabilities, subtract your liabilities from your assets and you will have your net worth.

Liabilities

CREDITOR	INTEREST RATE	OUTSTANDING BALANCE
Mortgage Loan	%	$
Bank Loan	%	$
Student Loan	%	$
Personal	%	$
Installment Debt	%	$
Credit Cards	%	$
Auto Loans	%	$
Other	%	$
TOTAL LIABILITIES		$

This is Where I Am Now Financially:
ASSETS – LIABILITIES = $

Increase Assets

Decrease Liabilities

This is Where I Want To Be Financially:

$ _____

34

TRACKING YOUR USE OF MONEY

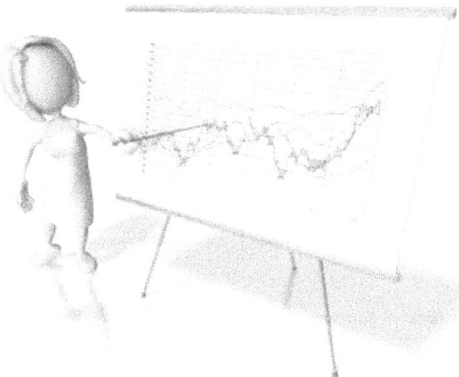

How do you plan to meet your money needs, wants, and goals?

Create A Money Tracking Plan.

Tracking expenses is a key aspect of maintaining the budget and achieving the financial goals you have created. If you do not track the use of your money, there is no way of knowing whether or not you are staying within the budget you have established.

For the next four weeks, track your use of money. The most basic tracking method involves writing all of your expenses in a notebook on a daily basis. We have provided a tracking sheet for you. If you choose to track your expenses in a notebook, it is important that you carry the notebook every where you go. Otherwise, you may forget to record an expense. When you're documenting your expenses, it may be easier to categorize your spending – living expenses, utilities, food, entertainment, gas, charity, etc.

Money Mastery Tip: If you want to track your use of money using receipts be sure to collect them on a daily basis. Then at the end of the week sort them into categories and add them up.

Goals

1. _____
2. _____
3. _____

YOUR MONEY TRACKING PLAN

Paid in Cash	Paid by Check or Debit Card	Automatic Payment from Bank Account

YOUR MONEY TRACKING PLAN

Paid in Cash	Paid by Check or Debit Card	Automatic Payment from Bank Account

YOUR MONEY TRACKING PLAN

Paid in Cash	Paid by Check or Debit Card	Automatic Payment from Bank Account

YOUR MONEY TRACKING PLAN

Paid in Cash	Paid by Check or Debit Card	Automatic Payment from Bank Account

Short Term Money Goals

Fill out the next two charts to plan on achieving your short term and long term goals as you use and enjoy your money.

Short Term Goals	Amount Needed	Month(s) Needed to achieve short term goal	Monthly savings needed
Ex. Save for a week vacation	$		$

Long Term Money Goals

Long Term Goals	Amount Needed	Month(s) Needed to achieve Long term goal	Monthly savings needed
Ex. Save 20% of annual income.	$		$

SAVING ACCOUNTS

One of the greatest ways to have your money work for you is to begin to save at least 20% of your earned or passive income. Have your bank deduct at least a 20% of your earned income and place in a separate account before you see it.

Put your money into a savings account, money market account, or certificate of deposit so that your money will gain interest. Shop around for the best rates.

Check to be sure that the bank is FDIC insured.

Types of Savings Accounts

Account Type	Description
Regular Savings	You deposit money at your discretion.
Savings Club	You deposit a fixed amount every week, bi-weekly, or monthly.
CDs (Certificates of Deposit)	You deposit a fixed amount that gains a determined amount of interest for a set period of time.
Money Market Account	You deposit a large amount, You receive interest and you may write a few checks each month.

HAVE YOU STARTED SAVING FOR RETIREMENT?

Savings for Retirement

It is important to create a retirement plan and begin saving and investing for the day you plan to retire and continue to maintain your desired lifestyle. There are a number of investment vehicles that have been specifically developed to foster your investment for retirement. When people have jobs, they are usually provided with some type of employer retirement plans including pension plans, 401k, 403b, etc. Contact your employer to participate in their retirement plan. Seek professional counsel in choosing the right investments for your retirement plan.

Questions you need to ask in regards to preparing financially for retirement.

How much do you need to save monthly?

How much money will need to retire comfortably?

What expenses do you expect to have when you retire?

What sources of income will you have?

Do you have an investment plan to reach your retirement goal?

Do you have a financial expert to help keep you on track?

Types of Retirement Accounts

401(k)	A variation of the profit-sharing and thrift plan. Employees make regular tax deferred contributions and the employers can match a portion or all of the employee's contributions.
403(b) Plans	Another variation of the profit sharing and thrift plan for non-profit organizations.
Thrift or Savings Plan	Contributions are made by both the employer and the employee where the employer can match all or a percentage of the employee's contributions.
Employee stock ownership plan (ESOP):	The employer contributes shares of the company's stock to employees in return for special tax benefits.
Money Purchase Pension Plan	A retirement plan with fixed-percentage compensations by the employers. Unlike profit sharing plans, these contributions are mandatory every year, regardless of profits.
Profit Sharing Plan	An employer alone makes contributions based on an employee's current-year compensation.
457 Plans	Are aimed at state and local government employees of tax-exempt organizations.
Pensions	Is a type of retirement plan that guarantees a specific amount to be paid out to the employee during retirement.
Annuities	Is a defined benefit plans that have fixed monthly payments at the age of retirement.
IRA	See next page for description.

There are several types of Individual Retirement Accounts:

Traditional IRA
The term used to define the regular IRA to participants under age 70 1/2. Annual contributions have a limit of $5,000 ($6,000 if you're age 50 or older). Earnings on the account are tax deferred until withdrawal, which must begin at age 70 1/2. Distributions are taxed at that time; if the distributions are not taken at that age, there is a 50% penalty on the amount not taken.

Roth IRA
Roth IRAs are similar to traditional IRAs, except that contributions come from after-tax earnings and are not taxed when withdrawn. After holding the Roth IRA account for a minimum of five years and reaching the age of 59 1/2, all withdrawals are tax-free, with the exception of gains. Seek professional counsel to see if you qualify.

Individual Retirement Annuity
A traditional or a Roth IRA established with a life insurance company through the purchase of a special annuity contract.

Simplified Employee Pension (SEP-IRA)
A traditional IRA established by an employer for employees. Employer contributions can be up to $40,000 or 25% of an employee's annual compensation.

Savings Incentive Matching Plan for Employers IRA (SIMPLE-IRA)
A traditional IRA established by small companies for employees. Participants can contribute up to $8,000 a year ($9,000 if age 50 or older); employers will match a portion of the employee's contribution.

Spousal IRA
A traditional or a Roth IRA set up by a married person in the name of his/her spouse. There is a $5,000 limit on Spousal IRA contributions. Couples must file jointly in that year. Seek professional advice to see if qualify.

Rollover or Conduit IRA
A traditional IRA established by an individual to receive a distribution from a qualified retirement plan, such as a 401(k). There is no limit on the contributions transferred to a rollover IRA.

Inherited IRA
A traditional or Roth IRA given to a non-spousal beneficiary of a deceased IRA owner.

Saving for Education

People save for education for different reasons. Some save and invest for the long term so that their children can go to college. Some save and invest for the short term so that so that they themselves may go back to get some form of higher education.

Types of Investments used for save for Future Education

CDS	$
U.S. Savings Bonds	$
Mutual Funds	$
Educational IRA	$
529 Plans	$
Investment Property	$

Tips on Saving for Education

Start early.

Add to your savings on a consistent monthly basis.

Make time a factor when choosing the type of investment vehicle so it matures when you need the money.

Keep in mind that if you do not choose to use the savings from some plans specifically designed for education i.e. (529 Plans) you may encounter the following drawbacks.

You will be penalized 10% when you withdraw the money and use it for something else. Also the state and the federal government will tax the earning from the 529 Plan from your current tax bracket. If there is any excess money in the 529 Plan that money may be penalized and taxed by the state and the federal government. In this case it is best to estimate slightly under what is needed to complete the education based on a four year term at the educational institution of choice.

INVESTMENTS

Investing is putting a portion of your money where you believe you will receive a **return on investment (ROI).** Before you consider investing you should seek financial counsel from an experienced professional.

After you have a strong financial foundation you may want to consider delving into the realm of investing.

Types of Investments

Stock - A type of security that signifies ownership in a corporation and represents a claim on part of the corporation's assets and earnings. There are two main types of stock: common and preferred. Common stock usually entitles the owner to vote at shareholders' meetings and to receive dividends. Preferred stock generally does not have voting rights, but has a higher claim on assets and earnings than the common shares.

Bond - A debt investment in which an investor loans money to an entity (corporate or governmental) that borrows the funds for a defined period of time at a fixed interest rate. Bonds are used by companies, municipalities, states and U.S. and foreign governments to finance a variety of projects and activities. Bonds are commonly referred to as fixed-income securities. Bonds can be divided into two types, taxable and tax-exempt.

Mutual Fund - An investment vehicle that is made up of a pool of funds collected from many investors for the purpose of investing in securities such as stocks, bonds, money market instruments and similar assets. Mutual funds are operated by money managers, who invest the fund's capital and attempt to produce capital gains and income for the fund's investors. A mutual fund's portfolio is structured and maintained to match the investment objectives stated in its prospectus.

Exchange Traded Funds - ETF's are funds that can be traded just like stocks on an exchange. Most ETF's track indices (S&P 500, Specific industries, etc) and usually include a bundle of securities who's performance is meant to mimic the performance of the index that the ETF is meant to track.

Commodities - A commodity is anything from gold, silver, or oil, to farm products, such as cotton, soybeans, or meat. It can also be foreign currencies, such as yen, pounds, and lira. The prices of commodities are driven mostly by supply and demand.

Collectible - A collectible is any physical asset that appreciates in value over time because it is rare or it is desired by many. A collectible is anything from baseball cards, coins, stamps, or dolls to antiques. When you buy these collectibles, you hope to resell them for a profit some day.

Annuities - An annuity is an insurance product that pays out income, and can be used as part of a retirement strategy. Annuities are a popular choice for investors who want to receive a steady income stream in retirement. There are two basic types of annuities: deferred and immediate. With a deferred annuity, your money is invested for a period of time until you are ready to begin taking withdrawals, typically in retirement. If you opt for an immediate annuity you begin to receive payments soon after you make your initial investment. For example, you might consider purchasing an immediate annuity as you approach retirement age. The deferred annuity accumulates money while the immediate annuity pays out.

Treasury Bills - Treasury bills, or T-bills, are sold in terms ranging from a few days to 52 weeks. Bills are typically sold at a discount from the par amount (also called face value). For instance, you might pay $990 for a $1,000 bill. When the bill matures, you would be paid $1,000. The difference between the purchase price and face value is interest.

Treasury Notes - Treasury notes, sometimes called T-Notes, earn a fixed rate of interest every six months until maturity. Notes are issued in terms of 2, 3, 5, 7, and 10 years.

Treasury Bonds - Treasury bonds pay a fixed rate of interest every six months until they mature. They are issued in a term of 30 years.

EE/E Savings Bonds - Series EE savings bonds are safe, low-risk savings products that pay interest based on current market rates for up to 30 years for bonds purchased May 1997 through April 30, 2005. Series EE bonds purchased May 2005 and after will earn a fixed rate of return.

I Savings Bonds - I Bonds are a low-risk, liquid savings product. While you own them they earn interest and protect you from inflation.

Real Estate as Investment
Real estate investing can be a very profitable business if handled properly. Real Estate is one of the most profitable of investments because of the need for housing and business locations. Property prices are affected by the market and can drop, but smart investors know that property rarely goes down in value and if it does, it usually rebounds. Some people buy property and then sell it solely for profit. Others rent out the property for a monthly cash flow. These people are called real estate investors.

Residential real estate
Investment in residential real estate is the most common form of real estate investment it includes property purchased as a primary residence or rental property.

Commercial real estate
Commercial real estate consists of multifamily apartments, office buildings, retail space, hotels and motels, warehouses, and other commercial properties.

Which of these investment vehicles do you currently have?

Savings Bonds	$
Annuities	$
Mutual Funds/ ETF	$
Bonds	$
Stocks	$
Real Estate	$
Commercial Real Estate	$
Collectibles	$
Commodities	$
Treasury Bills	$
Treasury Notes	$
Treasury Bonds	$
EE/E Savings Bonds	$
I Savings Bonds	$

INSURANCE

Insurance is defined as the equitable transfer of the risk of a loss, from one entity to another, in exchange for payment. An insurer is a company selling the insurance; the insured, or policyholder, is the person or entity buying the insurance policy. Having the proper insurance coverage is very important. It is a responsibility to our love ones to have insurance just for those unexpected life events. When you purchase insurance you are contracted to pay the premium and the insurance company agrees to pay the benefits upon meeting the contingencies of the contracted benefits. **If you do not currently have insurance, please contact an insurance expert.**

Types of Insurance

Health Insurance - Becoming more and more of a necessity as medical costs continue to rise. Health insurance can keep you from financial ruin if you encounter a health crisis.

- Accidental death and dismemberment insurance
- Dental insurance
- Disability insurance (Total permanent disability insurance)
- Income protection insurance
- Long term care insurance
- National health insurance
- Payment protection insurance
- Vision insurance

Life Insurance - Is highly recommended by experts because it is essential to sound financial planning. Life insurance is important for two reasons. One, it ensures that your family will enjoy the same standard of living after you die that they do now. Secondly, it will take care of your final expenses, such as funeral and burial costs.

- Permanent life insurance
- Term life insurance
- Universal life insurance
- Variable universal life insurance
- Whole life insurance

Residential Insurance- This insurance is usually required by your mortgage lender and is otherwise highly recommended. Homeowners insurance provides protection against damage to your home, theft, and litigation.

- Contents insurance
- Earthquake insurance
- Flood insurance
- Home insurance
- Landlords insurance
- Mortgage insurance
- Property insurance
- Title insurance

Vehicle Insurance - Vehicle insurance (also known as auto insurance, GAP insurance, car insurance, or motor insurance) is insurance purchased for cars, trucks, motorcycles, and other road vehicles. Its primary use is to provide financial protection against physical damage and/or bodily injury resulting from traffic collisions and against liability that could also arise. It can protect you from accident-related expenses, such as liability lawsuits and hospital stays.

- Aviation insurance
- Marine insurance
- Satellite insurance
- Travel insurance
- Vehicle insurance

Business Insurance – Insurance coverage that protects businesses from losses due to events that may occur during the normal course of business. By paying a relatively small premium to the insurance company, the business can protect itself against the possibility of sustaining a much larger financial loss. All businesses need to insure against risks—such as fire, theft, natural disaster, legal liability, automobile accidents, and the death or disability of employees.

- Bond insurance
- Directors and officers liability insurance
- Errors and omissions insurance
- Fidelity bond

- Professional indemnity insurance
- Professional liability insurance
- Protection and indemnity insurance
- Trade credit insurance
- Umbrella insurance

APPLYING THE WEALTH PRINCIPLES OF THE MONEY MASTERS

The approaches to wealth creation are different to a range of individuals. For some, real estate investments offer a steady inflow of tax advantages and cash. To others, the index funds of the stock market increases their nest. In addition, wealth means a number of different things to different individuals. For some, wealth means the capacity to pay for the college education of each of their children and leave them with legacy wealth. To others, it simply means the capacity to afford huge mansions, luxury cars and being able to have the time to do what they like. In spite of what you believe wealth represents and what approaches you use in wealth creation, according to Money Masters, there are actually four principles of wealth creation:

- Start early
- Make more
- Spend less
- Manage risks

Start Early

Compound interest is remarkable; if your predecessors had put away one dollar for you two hundred years in the past and the dollar earned 10 percent each year since then, your net worth as a result of that one dollar would be an astonishing $190,000,000+ today. In the event that you had invested $300 per month in S&P 500 index over the last 30 years, your net value of the total investment would now make you a millionaire. No matter where you are financially, today is always a good day to start saving.

Make More

For wealth building, it is of utmost importance to have an adequate amount of a nest egg to make your money grow regardless of the strategies that you choose to make use of; whatever it is either the stock market investment or real estate investing. There are essentially two methods of making more money from working your regular 9 to 5 job in addition to a secondary source of income. In addition to working experience and education, the industry in which you are sets the range on the amount that you will generate from a career.

Spend Less

Unless you control your spending through the use of a budget, you will not be able to create wealth. Too frequently individuals who generate a million dollars per year wind up with another million dollars in debt given that he or she uses two million dollars per year. Individuals who make $50,000 per year could save up to $10,000 if they keep their expenses under $40,000 per year. Having good wealth mentors will help.

Manage Risks

One unfortunate event in your life could wipe out years of saving if you had not put in place suitable life insurance, property insurance and health insurance. When you invest in real estate or the stock market there is risk involved. That's why it is very important to have strategies in place just case something changes in the market or with the real estate market. The ultimate goal in wealth creation is continue to build a legacy that you will pass from one generation to the next.

LIST 50 WAYS YOU CAN EARN ADDITONAL INCOME

**List 50 ways to put more money in your bank account.
Examples:**

1. Start your own business
2. Increase the amount of rental property that you own.
3. Increase the amount of rent you receive.

4. _____
5. _____
6. _____
7. _____
8. _____
9. _____
10. _____
11. _____
12. _____
13. _____
14. _____
15. _____
16. _____
17. _____

18. _____
19. _____
20. _____
21. _____
22. _____
23. _____
24. _____
25. _____
26. _____
27. _____
28. _____
29. _____
30. _____
31. _____
32. _____
33. _____
34. _____
35. _____

36. _____
37. _____
38. _____
39. _____
40. _____
41. _____
42. _____
43. _____
44. _____
45. _____
46. _____
47. _____
48. _____
49. _____
50. _____

YOUR MONEY EXPERIENCE

Day 1: Open two bank accounts: One for savings and the other for investing. Saving is another important key to financial success. You should work towards saving at least 20% percent of your income each month. This money will add up quickly, if you are consistent and persistent. Write a one-page journal on the experience. If you previously had a savings and investment account discuss the experience and your thoughts of the importance of both accounts. _____

_____
_____
_____
_____
_____
_____
_____
_____
_____
_____
_____
_____
_____
_____
_____
_____
_____
_____
_____
_____
_____
_____
_____
_____
_____
_____

Day 2: Get one hundred dollars and carry it in your wallet for 30 days. You are not allowed to use it. The purpose of the hundred dollars is to enhance your mindset that you can carry cash that belongs to you, and a part of your worth physically resides in your wallet. Keep a journal of this experience for the next thirty days. ***No matter what comes up, do not use the money!***

Day 3: Use cash to buy goods and services for the next thirty days. It is best if you have a debit card to withdraw the money. Then use paper cash to purchase what you need. The key to this plan of action is to know when you are going to use your money and stick to it. This will help you learn more about managing your money as well. Keep a journal of this experience for the next thirty days.

Day 4: Each week or every two weeks begin giving 10% of your income to a charitable organization. Next give 10% of your income to your investment fund. Last use the rest of your income to pay your monthly expenses. Journal this experience.

Day 5: Creatively write ways that you can produce more cash on a monthly basis. Then create ways that you can produce more cash on a daily basis. You are filled with money making ideas. Be creative! _____
_____
_____
_____
_____
_____
_____
_____
_____

Opportunities to increase cash daily/monthly
You can sell:
- Items
- Information
- Services
- Entertainment

Five ways I can creatively produce cash daily:

1. _____
2. _____
3. _____
4. _____
5. _____

Five ways I can creatively produce cash monthly:

1. _____
2. _____
3. _____
4. _____
5. _____

Day 6: Find an investment vehicle that you have not previously used to invest your cash. Investing allows you to grow your money at a much quicker rate. Be wise and seek the counsel of an experienced investor or money manager. From the words of John Addison *"Never take advice from someone more screwed up than you."* Many people invest money successfully on their own, but if you are just starting out, you may consider finding a financial planner to help you achieve your goals. Keep a journal of this experience.

Day 7: **Reflection:** How has your CASH ONLY lifestyle changed? How has it been enhanced? What areas do you need to continue working on? Keep a journal of your reflection.

BUILDING YOUR CREDIT HISTORY

For years, creditors have been using credit scoring systems to determine if you would be a good risk to loan money to for credit cards, auto loans, and mortgages. These days, many more types of businesses — including insurance companies and phone companies — are using credit scores to decide whether to approve you for a loan or service and on what terms. Auto and homeowners insurance companies are among the businesses that are using credit scores to help decide if you would be a good risk for insurance. A higher credit score means you are likely less of a risk, and in turn, means you will be more likely to get credit or insurance — or pay less for it.

The amended Fair Credit Reporting Act permits consumers to request a free copy of their credit report once every 12 months from each of the three major credit reporting agencies (i.e., Equifax, Experian, Trans Union).

What is credit scoring?

Credit scoring is a system creditors use to help determine whether to give you credit. It also may be used to help decide the terms you are offered or the rate you will pay for the loan.

The following areas are used to evaluate your "credit worthiness"
Have a steady verified income stream.
Pay your bills on time.
Have a steady checking account (no bounced checks).
Have a steady savings account (make regular deposits).

Credit Report Agencies Collect Information about your Credit Worthiness from:
Public records
Retail Stores
Credit Card Companies
Mortgage Companies and other Lenders
Student Loan Records

A credit reporting agency may share your credit information to anyone who plans to:
Lend you money

Issue you a credit card.
Hire for employment.
Sell you Life Insurance.
Rent you an apartment.

Bad Credit History
You cannot erase a bad credit history.
Most facts stay on your credit history for seven years.
If you file bankruptcy, it can be on your credit record for up to ten years.

Repair Bad Credit History
The most common and sensible manner to rebuild your credit history:
Begin paying above and beyond the balance on remaining revolving credit debt on time all the time.
Get a secured credit card.
You will know that your credit is secured with your own money. If you overdraft your account and it becomes delinquent, it will be closed and your security deposit will be seized.
These "safeguards" will activate a stronger level of financial discipline within your manner of handling your money.
Have a stable savings account that you are depositing regularly, will show creditors that you are stabilizing your personal finances.

Credit Reporting Agencies:

Equifax (www.equifax.com)
P.O. Box 740241
Atlanta, GA 30374-0241
1-800-685-1111

Experian (www.experian.com)
P.O. Box 2104
Allen, TX 75013-0949
1-888-EXPERIAN (397-3742)

Trans Union (www.transunion.com)
P.O. Box 1000
Chester, PA 19022
1-800-916-8800

USING CREDIT: OTHER PEOPLE'S MONEY

Credit is borrowing money. When you borrow money you have to pay back what you borrowed plus interest at an agreed time. In a loan, the borrower initially receives or borrows an amount of money, called the principal, from the lender, and is obligated to pay back or repay an equal amount of money to the lender at a later time. Typically, the money is paid back in regular installments, or partial repayments.

Types of Loans

Mortgages	A loan secured by the collateral of some specified real estate property which obliges the borrower to make a predetermined series of payments.
Bank Loans	Line of credit granted by a bank to a customer.
Credit Cards	Allows its holder to buy goods and services based on the holder's promise to pay for these goods and services.
Department Store Charge Card	Debt incurred on the charge account that will be paid in full and by due date.
Personal Loans	A sum borrowed from a certified lender either secured or unsecured loan
Automobile Loans	A loan used to purchase a vehicle.
Home Equity Loans	Is a type of loan in which the borrower uses the equity in their home as collateral.
Secured Loans	A loan that is secured against a valuable asset.
Unsecured Loans	A loan that does not use an asset as collateral.
Student Loans	A loan that is designed to help students pay for university tuition, books, and living expenses.

HOME OWNERSHIP

Is buying a home right for you? Buying a home has many benefits.

You will become part of a community, experience the security of owning the roof over your head, and have the opportunity to create a home that meets your needs and style. But before you purchase a home you must evaluate the pros and cons of homeownership.

Buying a Home

Pros	Cons
Owning property can be an investment. If you move, you may be able to sell it for a profit due to appreciation.	When you own a home, selling it before moving on is more complicated.
You control your home. You can redecorate, make improvements, extensions or rent it out.	You have to maintain the home and make repairs. You must maintain outside your home as well.
No one can increase your rent.	Your property taxes may increase.
You probably get more space for less money than if you rent.	Increased financial responsibility. You are responsible for all your utilities.
Pay for your home using cash you own it out right.	You probably need to take out a mortgage. This debt usually lasts 15 to 30 years.
The principal portion of every mortgage payment you make has the potential to grow your asset	If you are not financially prepared just in case of an emergency, you can lose your home.
Making on-time mortgage payments can help you create and keep up a strong credit history.	Missing a payment can affect your credit negatively.

Create A Plan of Action for Buying A Home.

You may want to think about the following considerations before buying your home:

- ➢ Additional financial responsibility. You will need to pay for maintenance and repairs. That's in addition to your mortgage payments, property taxes and homeowners insurance.

- ➢ Potential risk. Real estate often increases in value over time, but not always. Your property value can also go down.

- ➢ Bound by contract. As a renter, you can pick up and move with short notice. When you own a home, selling it before moving on is more complicated.

While owning a home has some wonderful advantages, it is one of the largest purchases most people make. Knowing what to expect as a homebuyer can help you make sound financial decisions.

*How will you fund the purchase of the home?*_____
_____
_____
_____

*What will the home look like? How many bedrooms and baths do you need?*_____
_____
_____
_____

Where will the home be located? Do you need to be in a particular school district, close to a job, public transportation, or day-care facility?
_____
_____
_____

*Do you have a Real Estate agent? Real estate agents make it their business to know about communities and the homes within them.*_____
_____
_____

Types of Mortgage Programs

There are a number of different mortgage rates available when you apply for a loan. The rate you receive will depend on a variety of circumstances and criteria. The amount of finance charges you pay during the life of your loan will be determined by your rate. A lower rate will enable you to pay less in finance charges. Before you sign any type of loan agreement, make sure you do your due diligence.

30 Year Fixed Rate Program

With a 30 year fixed rate program, the interest rate and mortgage payment remains fixed throughout the life of the loan for (360 months). A 30 year fixed rate mortgage is the most popular of all of the residential mortgage products and is available for conventional, jumbo, FHA, and VA loans.

15 Year Fixed Rate Program

Like a 30 year fixed rate program, a 15 year fixed rate program has an unchanging interest rate and monthly payment throughout the life of the loan this time at, (180 months). Typically, people choose a 15 year fixed rate program over a 30 year fixed rate program for the lower interest rate, a quicker mortgage payoff, and savings of more than half the total interest costs. Unfortunately, a 15 year fixed rate program carries a much higher monthly mortgage payment than that of a 30 year fixed rate program.

Adjustable Rate Program

An adjustable rate program differs in that the interest rate and the monthly payment are subject to adjustments, or resets. With an adjustable rate program, there is a generally an introductory or teaser period where the initial interest rate and monthly payment are low. Once the teaser period is over-- 1, 2, 3, 5, 7, or 10 years-- the loan goes through at least one reset a year where the interest rate changes. This interest rate change is based upon the initial margin and index.

FHA Program

The Federal Housing Administration (FHA) does not provide mortgage loans directly to individuals--they insure them for FHA-approved lenders. This insurance removes or minimizes default risk lenders face when borrowers put down less than 20 percent. In other words, FHA-backed loans helps lenders make it easier for low to moderate low-income families gain homeownership or refinance their current home loan.

VA Program (Department of Veterans Affairs)

Like FHA, the Department of Veterans Affairs (DVA) does not provide mortgage programs directly to individuals--they insure them for VA-approved lenders. VA loans are restricted to individuals that have served on active duty in the Air Force, Army, Coast Guard, Navy, or Marine Corps, and were discharged under conditions other than dishonorable. Visit the DVA website for further restrictions on eligibility. In addition to offering the 30 year fixed, 15 year fixed, and one year adjustable rate programs, the VA allows their eligible borrower a no-money down advantage for purchases.

Balloon Programs

Balloon programs are short term loans-- typically five or seven years-- that are amortized as if they are a 30 year fixed program. After the short term expires, the remainder of the balance is due in one lump sum or "balloon payment". Typically before the balloon payment reaches maturity, borrowers refinance or sell their property. In most cases, balloon programs have a refinance or conversion option that will allow the borrower to convert over to a fixed rate program after the short term has expired.

BUYING A CAR

Buy your car using cash, if you have saved for it.

Cars do not appreciate unless they are considered vintage so instead of paying interest on a depreciating item choose to use cash. If you have an old car, sell it yourself, you will probably get a better deal than if you trade it in.

New vs. Used Car... choose wisely

New Car: A new car will be at a higher price depending on make and model where the focus will be on maintenance rather than repairs.

Used Car: A used car will have a lower sticker price. But you may get a lemon and have to use a great deal of money on repairs. If you are buying a used car make sure you have the car inspected before you sign.

Shop around.
Negotiate for the best offer, if you are paying cash you have a negotiating advantage.

Leasing vs. Buying

Leasing, rather than buying a vehicle, can be a good option for some. If you lease, your monthly payments will be smaller than if you financed the purchase. Leasing, however, requires some contractual obligations, so it is not right for everyone. Make sure you review the contract for sale before signing. You do not want any hidden surprises.

CASHOLOGY The Science Of CASH ONLY Living

1) Live within your means. Try to save at least 20% of your net pay every pay period. Never live on a 100% of your pay. Do not be one paycheck away from a financial havoc.

2) Read financial publications such as; Wall Street Journal, New York Times, Forbes Magazine etc. Learn to look for opportunities and ways for your money to work for you instead of you working for your money. Gain financial **CASH ONLY** wisdom and take action.

3) Ask yourself before you make a purchase – is this a "want" or a "need." Listen to your inner voice and obey it when asking this important question. You may not always make the right decision, but at least take the time to think, before you make a purchase

4) Always have a long term goal for your money. Save and invest your money with a purpose; whether it is to buy a house as an investment property, purchase a business, or invest in stocks for retirement income.

5) Give a portion of your income to a nonprofit charity or your house of worship. You decide on an amount of money that you feel you can sow into these ministries. All that matters is that the amount be meaningful to you and you feel good about it.

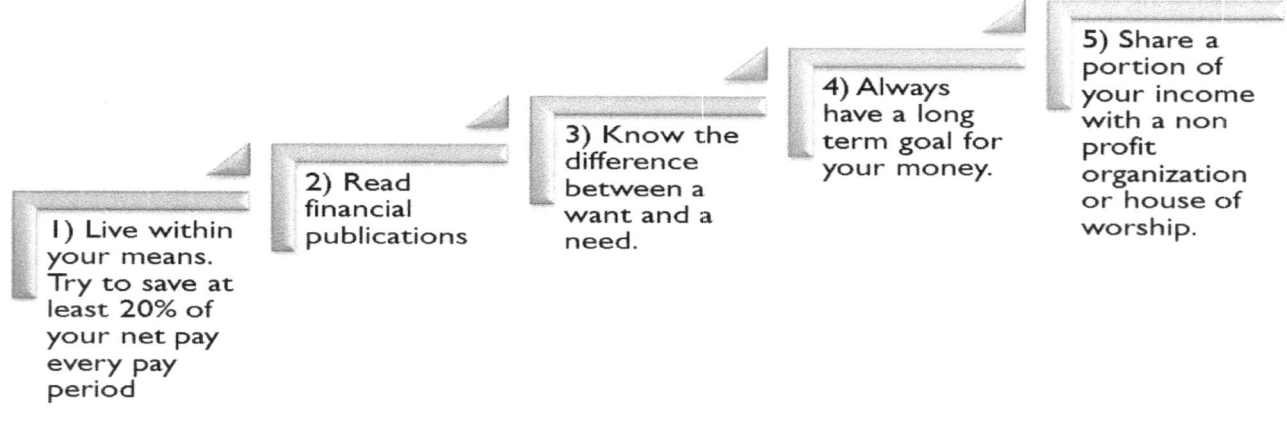

FINANCIAL TERMS

Here is a list of commonly used terms and their definitions in the investment and financial industries.

A

Accounts Payable — Money a company owes for services and supplies. For example, a record company would list as accounts payable the bill from a wax company that supplied the raw material for making records.

Accrued Interest — The interest due on a bond since the last interest payment was made. The buyer of the bond pays the market price plus accrued interest.

Acquisition — Acquiring control of one corporation by another. In "unfriendly" takeover attempts, the potential buying company may offer a price well above current market values, new securities and other inducements to stockholders. The management of the subject company might ask for a better price or try to join up with a third company.

ADR — American Depositary Receipt. A security issued by a U.S. bank in place of the Foreign shares held in trust by that bank, thereby facilitating the trading of foreign shares in U.S. markets.

After Tax Return — The yield of an investment after taxes have been taken out.

American Stock Exchange — The second largest stock exchange in New York, located in the financial district of New York City.

Amortization — Accounting for expenses or charges as applicable rather than as paid. Includes such practices as depreciation, depletion, write-off of intangibles, prepaid expenses and deferred charges.

Annual Report — The formal financial statement issued yearly by a publicly owned corporation. The report shows assets, liabilities, revenues, expenses and earnings. The report also shows the company's financial condition at the close of the business year and other basic information of interest to shareholders.

Annuity — An individual pays an insurance company a specified capital sum in exchange for a promise that the insurer will, at some time in the future, begin to make a series of periodic payments to the individual for as long as he/she lives or for some other specified period of time.

Appreciation — An increase in fair market value.

Asset — Anything a person, company, or group owns or is owed, including money, investments and property.

B

Balance Sheet — A condensed financial statement showing the nature and amount of a company's assets, liabilities and capital on a given date. In dollar amounts the balance sheet shows what the company owned, what it owed, and the ownership interest in the company of its stockholders.

Basis Point — One gradation on a 100-point scale representing one percent; used especially in expressing variations in the yields of bonds. Fixed income yields vary often and slightly within one percent and the basis point scale easily expresses these changes in hundredths of one percent.

Bear — Someone who believes the market will decline.

Bear Market — A condition of the stock market when prices of stocks are generally declining.

Beneficiary —- One who is designated to receive a benefit. Example: person who would receive the proceeds of a life insurance settlement.

Bid and Asked — The "bid" is the highest price anyone is willing to pay for a security at a given time; the "asked" is the lowest price anyone will take at that time. Stocks are usually purchased at "bid" and sold at "asked."

Blue-Chip Stock — Stock in a company with a national reputation for quality, reliability and the ability to operate profitably in good and bad times.

Bond — A promise of a corporation, municipality, government, church, and the like, to pay interest at a stated rate and repay face value of the bond which is actually a loan from you to the corporation or other entity at a specified maturity date.

Borrowing — A way of acquiring necessary capital. One form of borrowing is when an individual or a company asks a bank to loan them a certain amount of money, over a certain period of time, and agrees to pay a certain amount of interest.

Broker — An agent who handles the public's orders to buy and sell securities, commodities or other property. For this service a commission is charged.

Budget — A plan or guideline for spending.

Bull — One who believes the market will rise.

Bull Market — A condition of the stock market when prices of stocks are generally rising.

C

Capital Gain — Profit made on securities, either through dividends or by selling the securities for a higher price than they originally cost.

Capitalization — Total amount of various securities issued by a corporation. Capitalization may include bonds, debentures, preferred and common stock, and surplus.

Capital Needs — In personal financial planning, the amount of capital (assets or cash) needed in a lump sum to enable one to meet income needs and expenses should death or disability occur.

Cash Flow — The process of money coming in from various sources (income) and being spent on various uses (expenses). A cash flow statement is a look at both the income and the expenses over any period of time, but is usually for at least a month and/or a year.

Certificate — The actual piece of paper that is evidence of ownership of stock in a corporation. Watermarked paper is finely engraved with delicate etchings to discourage forgery.

Certificate of Deposit (CD) — An agreement with a bank that you will leave your money on deposit for a specified period of time in return for a specific amount of interest.

Collateral — Securities or other property pledged by a borrower to secure repayment of a loan.

Commercial Paper — Debt instruments issued by companies to meet short-term financing needs.

Commission — The broker's basic fee for purchasing or selling securities or property as an agent.

Common Stock — Securities that represent an ownership interest in a corporation. Generally have dividend and appreciation potential.

Corporate Bond — A bond issued by a corporation.

Current Assets — Those assets that can easily be converted into cash or sold in a short period of time. Example: stocks, certificates of deposit, cash value of life insurance, and money market funds; also known as liquid assets.

Current Liabilities — Money owed and payable by a company, usually within one year.

D

Day Order — An order to buy or sell which, if not executed, expires at the end of the trading day on which it was entered.

Debt — A sum owed to someone else, either a financial or personal obligation; a state of owing.

Debit Balance — In a customer's margin account, that portion of the purchase price of stock, bonds or commodities that is covered by credit extended by the broker to the margin customer.

Depreciation — Normally charges against earnings to write off the cost, less salvage value, of an asset over its estimated useful life. It is a bookkeeping entry and does not represent any cash outlay nor are funds earmarked for the purpose.

Discretionary Account — An account in which the customer gives the broker or someone else discretion to buy and sell securities or commodities including selection, timing, amount, and price to be paid or received.

Diversification — Spreading money among different types of investments.

Dividend — The payment designated by a corporation to be distributed pro rata among outstanding shares of stock. Corporations usually declare dividends from their profits, and the amount is in relation to the amount of the profit.

Dividend Election — The method you choose to receive your dividends. Most commonly refers to life insurance. You may elect dividends to be paid in cash, to reduce premiums, to buy paid-up additions, or to accumulate at interest.

Dollar Cost Averaging — A method of purchasing securities at regular intervals with a fixed amount of dollars, regardless of the prevailing prices of the securities. Payments buy more shares when the price is low and fewer shares when it rises.

E

Earnings Report — A statement – also called an income statement – issued by a company showing its earnings or losses over a given period. The earnings report lists the income earned, expenses and the net result.

Economic Indicator — A key statistic in the overall economy that experts use as a yardstick to predict the performance of the stock market.

Effective Rate — The amount of each dollar earned that goes to pay taxes. The ratio of total taxes paid to gross income.

Equity — The ownership interest of common and preferred stockholders in a company.

Exercise — Action taken by an option holder that requires the writer to perform the terms of the contract.

Exercise Prices — The prices at which an option may be exercised. Also called strike prices.

Expiration Date — The date the option contract expires.

F

Face Value — The value of a bond that appears on the face of the bond, unless the value is otherwise specified by the issuing company. Face value is ordinarily the amount the issuing company promises to pay at maturity. Face value is not an indication of market value.

Fair Market Price — A reasonable price for securities based on supply and demand.

Fiduciary — One who acts for another in financial matters.

Financial Futures — Futures contracts based on financial instruments such as U.S. Treasury bonds, CDs and other interest-sensitive issues, currencies and stock market indicators.

Fiscal Year — A corporation's accounting year. Due to the nature of that particular business, some companies do not use the calendar year for their bookkeeping.

Floor — The huge trading area where stocks are bought and sold on the New York Stock Exchange.

Floor Brokers — The largest single membership group of the NYSE. There are two main types: Commission brokers, employed by brokerage houses, buy and sell securities on the NYSE floor for the general public. Independent floor brokers work for themselves. They execute orders for brokerages without full-time commission brokers or for overly busy brokers.

Free and Open Market — A market in which supply and demand are freely expressed in terms of price. Contrasts with a controlled market in which supply, demand and price may all be regulated.

Fundamental Research — Analysis of industries and companies based on such factors as sales, assets, earnings, products or services, markets and management. As applied to the economy, fundamental research includes consideration of gross national product, interest rates, unemployment, inventories, savings, etc.

Futures — A contract specifying a future date of delivery or receipt of a certain amount of a specific tangible or intangible product. The commodities traded in futures markets include stock index futures; agricultural products like wheat, soybeans and pork bellies; metals; and financial instruments.

G

Good 'Til Canceled (GTC) — Order An order to buy or sell at a specific price until the investor cancels the order.

Going Public — When a company sells shares of itself to the public to raise capital.

Government Bond — A bond issued by the federal government.

Growth Stock — Stock of a company with a record of earnings growth at a relatively high rate.

H

Hedging — The purchase or sale of a derivative security (such as options or futures) in order to reduce or neutralize all or some portion of the risk of holding another security.

Holding Company — A corporation that owns the securities of another, in most cases with voting control.

I

Income Statement — A report on a company's financial status over a period of time. It totals profits subtracts expenses and pinpoints how much money the company can reinvest.

Income Stock — Common stocks that pay large dividends that an investor could use as income.

Index — A statistical yardstick expressed in terms of percentages of a base year or years. For instance, the NYSE Composite Index of all NYSE common stocks is based on yea r-end 1965 as 50. An index is not an average.

Individual Retirement Account (IRA) — A retirement provision established by law that allows an individual to deduct from his income a certain amount set aside for future retirement.

Inflation —- An increase in the volume of money and credit relative to available goods resulting in a substantial and continuing rise in the general price level.

Inflation Rate — An important economic indicator; the rate at which prices are rising.

Initial Public Offering (IPO) — A corporation's first offering of stock to the public.

Investment - The use of money for the purpose of making more money: to gain income, increase capital, save taxes, or a combination of-the three.

Investment Portfolio — A variety of securities owned by an individual or an institution.

Issue — Any of a company's securities, or the act of distributing such securities.

K

Keogh Plan — Tax advantaged personal retirement program that can be established by a self-employed individual.

L

Liabilities — All the claims against a corporation. Liabilities include accounts, wages and salaries payable; dividends declared payable; accrued taxes payable; fixed or long-term liabilities, such as mortgage bonds, debentures and bank loans. (see Assets, Balance Sheet)

Limit Order — An order to buy or sell when and if a security reaches a specific price.

Liquidate — When a company fails, the process of converting all of its assets back into cash and distributing it to those with a claim on it.

Liquidity — How easily one's assets can be converted back into cash. Liquidity is one of the m o s t important characteristics of a good market.

Long-Term Assets — Those assets that cannot easily be converted to cash or sold or consumed in a short period of time. Example: home, real estate, and land assets.

M

Margin — The amount paid by the customer when using a broker's credit to buy or sell a security. Under Federal Reserve regulations, the initial margin required since 1934 has ranged from 40% of the purchase price up to 100%. Since 1974 the current rate of 50% has been in effect.

Market Order — An order to buy or sell at the best price currently available on the Trading Floor.

Market Price — The last reported price at which the stock or bond sold, or the current quote

Maturity Date — The date that a bond comes due and must be paid off.

Merger — A combination of two or more corporations.

Minimum Deposit — When the cash value increases in the insurance policy are used to pay the premiums of the policy.

Mortgage — Usually refers to the balance of the loan on a home. The amount of money borrowed to purchase a home.

Money Market Account — An account in which your money is reinvested in short-term securities by the bank or investment firm managing the account.

Money Market Fund — A mutual fund whose investments are in high-yield money market instruments such as federal securities, CDs and commercial paper. Its intent is to make such instruments, normally purchased in large denominations by institutions, available indirectly to individuals.

Mortgage Bond — A bond secured by a mortgage on a property. The value of the property may or may not equal the value of the bond issued against it.

Municipal Bond — A bond issued by a county, city, district or authority.

N

NASD — The National Association of Securities Dealers, an association of brokers and dealers in the over-the-counter securities business.

Nasdaq — An automated New York Stock Exchange information network that (NYSE) — The largest provides brokers and dealers organized securities market in with price quotations on the United States, founded in securities traded over- t h e 1792.

NonLiquid — Investments not easily converted to cash at their current fair market value.

O

Offer — The price at which a person is ready to sell. Opposed to bid, the price at which one is ready to buy.

Options — A right to buy or sell a fixed amount of a given stock at a specified price within a limited period of time. If the right is not exercised the option expires and the buyer forfeits the money.

Orders — Specific instructions for handling transactions.

Over-The-Counter (OTC) — A market for securities made up of dealers who may or may not be members of a securities exchange. The OTC market is conducted over the telephone and deals mainly with stocks of companies without sufficient shares, stockholders or earnings to warrant listing on an exchange.

P

Par — Equal to the nominal or face value of a security.

Preferred Stock — Similar to common stock. Generally less dividend and appreciation potential but receives a higher priority or preference over common stock in dividend payments or in the event of liquidation.

Premium — The payment an insurance policy holder agrees to make for coverage.

Present Value — The value of a sum of money to be received in the future in today's dollars taking into account either interest rates, inflation, or both.

Prime Rate — The interest rate charged by large U. S. money center commercial banks to their best business borrowers.

Principle — A person's capital or money. Used for investments. Sometimes referred to as equity when talking about a house.

Prospectus — A circular that describes securities or investments being offered for sale to the public.

Proxy — Written authorization given by a shareholder to someone else to represent him and vote his shares at a shareholder's meeting .

Proxy Statement — Information given to stockholders in conjunction with the solicitation of proxies.

Purchasing Power - The ability of a dollar to buy a product or service. As prices increase, purchasing power decreases.

Q

Quote — The highest bid to buy and the lowest offer to sell any stock at a given time.

R

Rate of Return — In stocks and bonds, the amount of money returned to investors on their investments. Also known as y i e l d.

Recession — A period of no or negative economic growth and high unemployment.

Refinancing — Same as refunding. New securities are sold by a company and the money is used to retire existing securities. Object may be to save interest costs, extend the maturity of the loan, or both.

Reinvest — Funneling of profits back into a company to enhance its operations. An individual stockowner can also reinvest by designating that dividends paid on stock will be used to purchase additional shares of that stock.

REIT — Real Estate Investment Trust, an organization similar to an investment company in some respects but concentrating its holdings in real estate investments. The yield is generally liberal since REITs are required to distribute as much as 90% of their income.

Retained Earnings — Profits a company keeps for its operations, after paying taxes and dividends.

Right to vote — The right of common stockholders to vote on matters of corporate policy at an annual stockholder's meeting.

S

SEC — The Securities and Exchange Commission, established by Congress to help protect investors. The SEC administers the Securities Act of 1933, the Securities Exchange Act of 1934, the Securities Act Amendment of 1975, the Trust Indenture Act, the Investment Company Act, the Investment Advisers Act, and the Public Utility Holding Company Act.

Securities and Exchange Commission (SEC) — A watchdog agency created by the U.S. Congress to monitor the securities industry and enforce punishments of those that violate the industry's regulations.

Securities Investors Protection Corporation (SIPC) — A safeguard for investors capital created by Congress. The SIPC insures that cash and securities on deposit with a brokerage are insured up to $500,000 per customer, in the event that the brokerage goes out of business.

Stockholders' Equity — The value of all the stock owned by the shareholders of a particular company. Also known as net worth.

Syndicate — A group of investment bankers who together underwrite and distribute a new issue of securities or a large block of an outstanding issue.

T

Ticker — A telegraphic system that continuously provides the last sale prices and volume of securities transactions on exchanges. Information is either printed or displayed on a moving tape after each trade.

Treasuries — Debt obligations of the U.S. government. Treasuries are among the safest investments, since they are secured by the full faith and credit of the government. The interest of Treasuries is exempt from state and local taxes but is subject to federal income tax. There are three types of treasuries: Treasury Bills, with maturities of one year or less; Treasury Notes, with maturities ranging from one to 10 years; and Treasury Bonds, long-term instruments with maturities of 10 years or more.

Treasury Stock — Stock issued by a company but later reacquired. It may be held in the company's treasury indefinitely, reissued to the public, or retired. Treasury stock receives no dividend and has no vote while held by the company.

U

Unlisted Stock — A security not listed on a stock exchange.

V

Variable Annuity — A life insurance policy where the annuity premium (a set amount of dollars) is immediately turned into units of a portfolio of stocks. Upon retirement, the policyholder is paid accordingly to accumulated units, the dollar value of which varies according to the performance of the stock portfolio. Its objective is to enhance, through stock investment, the purchasing value of the annuity which otherwise is subject to erosion through inflation.

W

Will — The directions of a testator (the male or female who makes a will) regarding the final disposition of his or her estate.

Withholding — Refers to the amount of tax withheld from a paycheck.

Working Capital — The assets a company has that can be poured into the company's operations.

Y

Yield — In stocks and bonds, the amount of money returned to investors on their investments. Also known as rate of return.

Yield to Maturity — The yield of a bond to maturity takes into account the price discount from or premium over the face amount. It is greater than the current yield when the bond is selling at a discount and less than the current yield when the bond is selling at a premium.

Z

Zero Coupon Bond — A bond which pays no interest but is priced, at issue, at a discount from its redemption price.

Hasheem Francis is the Chairman and CEO of Built To Prosper Companies.
Hasheem Francis is an entrepreneur, investor, best-selling author, keynote speaker, recognized industry thought leader, and an expert on executive business and leadership development. With two decades of entrepreneurial and leadership experience, Hasheem Francis is a leadership consultant and advisor to CEOs, business leaders, corporate executives, and community leaders across the country. His vast expertise in dealing with business change, along with his strong financial investment background and leadership development skills, enables him to provide unique and unparalleled counsel to a diverse range of industry professionals. Hasheem has served as a founder, partner, CEO, CFO, and leadership consultant for a diverse range of entrepreneurial and mature companies.

Deborah Francis is the COO and President of Built To Prosper Companies.
Deborah is an entrepreneur, best-selling author, investor, keynote speaker, recognized industry thought leader, and an expert on business development. Deborah Francis has developed curriculums and delivered training sessions on entrepreneurship, small business development, and professional development. Deborah has trained, led and mentored hundreds of people with her functional knowledge and educational background. Deborah has a Masters in Secondary Education of English.

Deborah owns or holds interests in businesses operating in Leadership and Business Consulting, Legal and Identity Theft Services, Health and Wellness, Real Estate Investment, Book Publishing, Sports and Entertainment. Deborah Francis Companies is headquartered in Orlando, FL, with affiliate operations in New York, NY, and Hilton Head, SC.

Books by Hasheem Francis & Deborah Francis:

Built To Prosper
Built To Prosper For Women
Built To Prosper For Finances
Built To Prosper Women of Wisdom Journal
Built To Prosper Wealth of Wisdom Journal
The Joy of Healthy Living; The Guide To Eating Right For Life
Cashology The Science of Living A Cash Only Life
Cashology Academy Wealth Work
Cashology Academy Wealth Journal
Undeniable Confidence
The Science of Getting Rich: The Key To Peace, Power, & Prosperity

BUILT TO PROSPER
COMPANIES
CREATED BY VISIONARIES AND BUILT BY LEADERS

Built To Prosper Companies is an innovative business network that provides strategic consulting in a diverse portfolio of companies. As a leading provider of business consulting and training since 1999, **Built To Prosper Companies** has worked with over 1500 small to medium sized businesses. Built To Prosper Companies specializes in business: planning, marketing, leadership development, and organizational sales training. We equip entrepreneurs, senior leaders and business advisors across 110 countries with the insights and actionable solutions they need to respond quickly to evolving business conditions and transform operations.

"The business that is truly successful helps other businesses succeed. There are not many successful hermits." **Hasheem Francis, Chairman and CEO**

As the leading provider of consulting and training in the business services industry, **Built To Prosper Companies** produces value and unparalleled results for companies by delivering business solutions that support them in driving revenue growth. This is done with an uncompromising commitment toward serving our clients with the utmost respect, integrity, and the highest standards of excellence. Our delivery model is predicated on exacting alignment with the unique aspects of each client's business strategy, organizational structure and culture, ensuring each client engagement provides clear and actionable tactics that will drive success on an ongoing, quantifiable basis.

We believe that by delivering on this promise, we will help our clients not only drive incremental revenue growth, but also bring more meaning and fulfillment to our clients, their business, and the clients they serve.

Built To Prosper Companies is headquartered in Orlando, FL, with affiliate operations in New York, NY and Hilton Head, SC.

Visit us: www.BuiltToProsperCompanies.com

BUILT TO PROSPER SEMINARS will give you proven strategies to sharpen your leadership skills, business skills, financial and investment knowledge, relationships, spiritual life, and enjoy a healthy lifestyle.

Trainings & Seminars By BUILT TO PROSPER SEMINARS

Built To Prosper U
Cashology Academy
Loyal Leaders Seminar
The Joy Of Healthy Living
Young Entrepreneur's Academy
Emerging Business Boot Camp

We have a team of specialists who specialize in taking care of all our events and making sure we fully understand your needs as an organization. We have been producing amazing results for our clients and seminar participants for over a decade. **If you are interested in bringing Built To Prosper Seminars to your city, please send all request to:**

info@BTPCompanies.com

***Built To Prosper Mentoring*® Programs** are designed to empower you with the training, focus and accountability you need to achieve the consistent results you demand in the most important areas of your life. In order to succeed at the game of life, you must take action. We promise an experience that will not only stretch you, but that will be more fun than you have ever imagined possible. It is time you get the results in your life. Our programs are designed to address specific areas of personal and professional development.

Visit us: www.BTPMentoring.com

Our business mentors specialize in helping corporations, business owners, & entrepreneurs excel. Our business mentors are successful leaders in their respective businesses and have decided to mentor others.

Your Mentor will challenge you to:

* Develop a clear vision for your business
* Learn the secrets to enjoying a better work-life balance
* Develop key habits for continuing success
* How to build a profitable business
* Implement reflection and evaluation processes for continuous improvement
* Create a marketing plan to get better results for your products or services

Business Mentoring includes:

* Personal Business Consultant
* **(2) one-hour mentoring sessions a month (3 month commitment)**
* Company assessment
* Quarterly evaluation of business goals
* A Visionary Business Plan

Visit Built To Prosper Mentoring© program For A FREE Consultation www.BTPMentoring.com

Our leadership mentors specialize in training community leaders, corporate leaders, pastors, business leaders and managers, in how to accelerate the achievement of their professional and personal goals. Our leadership mentors are successful leaders in their respective industries and have decided to mentor others.

With the help of a Mentor, you can:

* Become an effective leader on the inside
* Learn how to be more consistent in your leadership activities
* Develop the influence to motivate your organization to higher levels of performance
* Learn to balance your work and time with the important people in your life
* Understand the power of leading by example

Leadership Mentoring includes:

* Personal Mentoring Consultant
* **(2) one hour mentoring sessions a month (3 month commitment)**
* Personalized behavioral assessment
* A copy of **Built To Prosper The Principles of Self Mastery**
* Leadership achievement system package

Our wealth mentors specialize in helping people achieve their maximum income earning potential by learning essential techniques to accumulating wealth. Our mentors have hands-on experience with building wealth, they are successful in their respective businesses and have decided to mentor others.

With the help of a Mentor, you can:

* Recognize and overcome your limited beliefs about wealth
* Learn proven techniques to the right money habits
* Be held accountable
* Apply the financial principles of the wealthy
* Create a legacy for your future generation

Wealth Mentoring includes:

* Personal Mentoring Consultant
* **(2) one hour mentoring sessions a month (3 month commitment)**
* A copy of Cashology Academy Wealth Workbook
* A copy of Cashology The Science of How To Live A Cash Only Life.
* A copy of The Cashology Academy Wealth Journal.

Our health mentors specialize in helping people experience the joy of healthy living. Our mentors are respected leaders in the health and wellness industry and have decided to mentor others.

Your Mentor will challenge you to:

* Develop a clear vision for your health
* Learn the importance of exercising
* Eat more fruits and vegetables
* Implement reflection and evaluation processes for continuous improvement
* Relax more and overcome excessive stress

Health Mentoring Includes:

* Personal Health Consultant
* **(2) one hour mentoring sessions a month (3 month commitment)**
* A copy of The Joy Healthy Living Book
* The E-course: 21 Days To A Healthier You
* Phone and Email Support From Health Consultant

Visit Built To Prosper Mentoring© program For A FREE Consultation www.BTPMentoring.com

BTP Publishing Group, is a pioneer in inventory book publishing, printing, fulfillment and distribution. We continue to expand our inventory book fulfillment network, allowing publishers and authors to seamlessly distribute their content through existing channels, as well as to leading retailers, e-tailers, distributors and other specialty book sales markets.

BTP Publishing Group provides professional services that enable authors to publish their own work, and by doing so, allows authors to retain control of their books' sales strategies and their profits.

Our Services
Offering a wide range of services from professional book interior and exterior design to editing and promotional tools, thousands of authors have taken advantage of our Unique Publishing System platform and expert staff to make their dreams a reality.

For more information visit: www.BTPPublish.com

www.ingramcontent.com/pod-product-compliance
Lightning Source LLC
Chambersburg PA
CBHW080521110426
42742CB00017B/3189